The Jig Is Up,
God!

spiritual journal and workbook

108
mind-blowing
consciousness-blasting
awareness-expanding
self-realizing
ego-reducing
spiritual hacks

YARON

cova tombol

ISBN 10: 9659116209
ISBN 13: 978-9659116201

Dear One,

With tremendous esteem and gratitude, I welcome and honor you as you travel on your spiritual path to discover your true self. This is one stop in your journey. A visit that I hope will be enjoyable and bear you sweet fruit.

After having searched for God for such a long time and in so many places, I feel I have finally found God. After God had been so elusive to me, as if hiding from me, I feel I have finally discovered God's hideout. Through doing spiritual practices, reading spiritual texts, and receiving spiritual guidance, God could no longer conceal Himself from me. In reality, God was not hidden from me at all. I discovered that God is standing right in front me, resting inside my mind, dwelling in my heart. I've got you cornered, God. The jig is up!

As you may already know, in order for our spiritual journey to bear fruit we require two ingredients: grace and effort. One supports and sustains the other. Grace is the divine generosity with which we have already been blessed. Our souls have been blessed with the ability to tell the difference between what brings us closer to and what takes us farther from understanding, knowing and ultimately realizing our own divine nature. It is grace that also makes us decide to make the necessary effort to bring more grace into our lives.

Effort is what we bring into our own spiritual journey. When we do spiritual practices, such as meditation, singing the glory of God, selflessly serving causes for improving our world, giving and sharing, and keeping graceful company, we generate a power that helps us to know our divine nature. This knowledge acts as a channel for receiving even more grace. Effort is its own reward. Contemplation is another very important spiritual practice that greatly helps us on our spiritual journey.

Suggested techniques on how to contemplate with the 5 Principles of "The Jig Is Up, God!"

Contemplation is a relatively easy spiritual practice. You can do it practically anywhere and anytime you feel like it. You can contemplate while comfortably sitting in a chair or under a tree as you watch the clear blue skies. You can also contemplate while doing sports, washing dishes or engaging in your favorite activity. And since each soul is different, do what comes naturally to you and what is comfortable for you.

But don't be fooled by its seeming simplicity -- contemplation is an incredibly powerful spiritual tool, one that can fill your soul with the wonderful feeling of contentment, make your spirit soar in grace-filled flight, and bring your mind to a smooth landing -- or not so smooth. After contemplating, however, you will always feel you have traveled farther on your spiritual path towards your home and ultimate goal, the reward of all your effort, the summit of existence, your own divine nature and true self -- Love -- to see God in all.

In "The Jig Is Up, God!" spiritual journal and workbook you will be requested to read the 5 principles of "The Jig Is Up, God!" Then you will read the statement you wish to contemplate. You may read it silently or out loud. You may begin by taking a few deep breaths, to help you focus. You may wish to take a few more deep breaths after reading the statement. You may choose to close your eyes for a few minutes. Hold the statement in your awareness. Hold it in your mind. Think it. Ask yourself how what meaning the statement takes on in view of the 5 Principles. Explore the meaning of statement in light of the 5 Principles. You may break up the statement into smaller parts. You can emphasize certain components of the statement. You can try changing the sequence of the words. You can put the statement in the form of a question. I also recommend to look up words in a dictionary and thesaurus. You can use your own technique for contemplation. Whatever works for you.

As you hold a contemplative thought that you feel is relevant to you and gain a certain insight, write them down in the space provided in the journal. Spaces are provided on each page for writing down your contemplations, your insights and your images.

Your own insights will allow you to further contemplate and discover your true self. Please visit www.TheJigIsUpGod.com for examples on how to contemplate within the context of the 5 principles of "The Jig Is Up, God!" spiritual journal and workbook.

A simple contemplation exercise – the human body as metaphor for God

The human body as a metaphor for God can make it easier to understand the nature of the soul in its relation to God. Let's take a quick moment to do a simple contemplation exercise. When you want to let someone know that it is you who did or said something, you usually point to your chest and say "Me." So, pointing to one part of your body lets it be known that you actually mean your entire body.

Pointing to your chest as if saying "Me" is a symbolic gesture. This gesture comes naturally to us, since the heart of our soul is located in the center of our chest. Now point with your finger to any other part of your body. For instance, you can point to your big toe. Depending on your point of view, you can either consider that you are simply pointing to your big toe or that you are pointing to your entire body.

Since, just like your chest, your big toe is a part of your body, then pointing to your big toe means that you are pointing to your entire body. Within the spiritual context, pointing to yourself means that you are actually pointing to God. Moreover, since "God is All," pointing anywhere means that you are actually pointing to God.

It is my sincere wish that you will apply the powerful tool of contemplation in your spiritual journey and gain the ultimate insight to your true divine self.

As part of your spiritual effort of journaling, you are to contemplate the 108 spiritual hacks provided in The Jig Is Up, God! in light of the following 5 Principles:

God is One

God is All

God is Love

God is Great

I am God

The 5 Principles of The Jig Is Up, God! are explained in the following manner:

God is One: God is the only entity that exists

God is All: God is every one and every thing

God is Love: God is Unity

God is Great: God is Joy

I am God: Awareness is God

My best wishes for success in discovering your true self and realizing your divine nature.

Love and light,

Yaron

The
Jig
Is
Up,
God!

All speech is monologue.

God is All, God is One, God is Love, God is Great, I am God.

My divine contemplation:
My divine insight:
My divine image:

All meals fill one stomach.

God is All, God is One, God is Love, God is Great, I am God.

My divine contemplation:

My divine insight:

My divine image:

All insult is self-deprecation.

God is All, God is One, God is Love, God is Great, I am God.

My divine contemplation:

My divine insight:

My divine image:

All killing is suicide.

God is All, God is One, God is Love, God is Great, I am God.

My divine contemplation:

My divine insight:

My divine image:

God is evolution.

God is All, God is One, God is Love, God is Great, I am God.

My divine contemplation:

My divine insight:

My divine image:

All sex is masturbation.

God is All, God is One, God is Love, God is Great, I am God.

My divine contemplation:
My divine insight:
My divine image:

Evolution is reincarnation.

God is All, God is One, God is Love, God is Great, I am God.

My divine contemplation:

My divine insight:

My divine image:

Science is nostalgia.

God is All, God is One, God is Love, God is Great, I am God.

My divine contemplation:
My divine insight:
My divine image:

There is no such thing as relativity.

God is All, God is One, God is Love, God is Great, I am God.

My divine contemplation:

My divine insight:

My divine image:

$$\heartsuit = E^{\infty}$$

(Love is Energy to the power of Infinity)

God is All, God is One, God is Love, God is Great, I am God.

My divine contemplation:

My divine insight:

My divine image:

The sum of all equations is one.

God is All, God is One, God is Love, God is Great, I am God.

My divine contemplation:

My divine insight:

My divine image:

Now has always been.

God is All, God is One, God is Love, God is Great, I am God.

My divine contemplation:

My divine insight:

My divine image:

I am the Big Bang Theory.

God is All, God is One, God is Love, God is Great, I am God.

My divine contemplation:

My divine insight:

My divine image:

I pull gravity.

God is All, God is One, God is Love, God is Great, I am God.

My divine contemplation:

My divine insight:

My divine image:

Love is seeing yourself in all.

God is All, God is One, God is Love, God is Great, I am God.

My divine contemplation:

My divine insight:

My divine image:

Love is at the core of all atoms.

God is All, God is One, God is Love, God is Great, I am God.

My divine contemplation:

My divine insight:

My divine image:

Love moves faster than the speed of light.

God is All, God is One, God is Love, God is Great, I am God.

My divine contemplation:

My divine insight:

My divine image:

God senses God.
(God sees God, God hears God, God touches God, God tastes God, God smells God)

God is All, God is One, God is Love, God is Great, I am God.

My divine contemplation:

My divine insight:

My divine image:

God performs God.
(God procreates God, God speaks God, God handles God, God excretes God, God moves God)

God is All, God is One, God is Love, God is Great, I am God.

My divine contemplation:
My divine insight:
My divine image:

All languages are synonymous.

God is All, God is One, God is Love, God is Great, I am God.

My divine contemplation:

My divine insight:

My divine image:

All words spell God.

God is All, God is One, God is Love, God is Great, I am God.

My divine contemplation:
My divine insight:
My divine image:

God spelled backwards is still God.

God is All, God is One, God is Love, God is Great, I am God.

My divine contemplation:
My divine insight:
My divine image:

God is the Supreme Webmaster.

God is All, God is One, God is Love, God is Great, I am God.

My divine contemplation:

My divine insight:

My divine image:

I am a divine website.

God is All, God is One, God is Love, God is Great, I am God.

My divine contemplation:

My divine insight:

My divine image:

I am on TV.

God is All, God is One, God is Love, God is Great, I am God.

My divine contemplation:

My divine insight:

My divine image:

I am social media.

God is All, God is One, God is Love, God is Great, I am God.

My divine contemplation:

My divine insight:

My divine image:

I am the gold mine of Love.

God is All, God is One, God is Love, God is Great, I am God.

My divine contemplation:

My divine insight:

My divine image:

I need no introduction.

God is All, God is One, God is Love, God is Great, I am God.

My divine contemplation:

My divine insight:

My divine image:

I am divine concentrate.

God is All, God is One, God is Love, God is Great, I am God.

My divine contemplation:

My divine insight:

My divine image:

The ego is God pretending not to know it is God.

God is All, God is One, God is Love, God is Great, I am God.

My divine contemplation:

My divine insight:

My divine image:

God is convincing.

God is All, God is One, God is Love, God is Great, I am God.

My divine contemplation:

My divine insight:

My divine image:

Movement is mirror.

God is All, God is One, God is Love, God is Great, I am God.

My divine contemplation:
My divine insight:
My divine image:

Action means swapping places.

God is All, God is One, God is Love, God is Great, I am God.

My divine contemplation:

My divine insight:

My divine image:

One Size Fits All.

God is All, God is One, God is Love, God is Great, I am God.

My divine contemplation:
My divine insight:
My divine image:

God is reading this.

God is All, God is One, God is Love, God is Great, I am God.

My divine contemplation:

My divine insight:

My divine image:

You are the Word.

God is All, God is One, God is Love, God is Great, I am God.

My divine contemplation:

My divine insight:

My divine image:

Every word means me.

God is All, God is One, God is Love, God is Great, I am God.

My divine contemplation:

My divine insight:

My divine image:

I am a know-it-all.

God is All, God is One, God is Love, God is Great, I am God.

My divine contemplation:
My divine insight:
My divine image:

There is no giving.

God is All, God is One, God is Love, God is Great, I am God.

My divine contemplation:

My divine insight:

My divine image:

There is no taking.

God is All, God is One, God is Love, God is Great, I am God.

My divine contemplation:

My divine insight:

My divine image:

There is no receiving.

God is All, God is One, God is Love, God is Great, I am God.

My divine contemplation:

My divine insight:

My divine image:

Only Love.

God is All, God is One, God is Love, God is Great, I am God.

My divine contemplation:

My divine insight:

My divine image:

We is.

God is All, God is One, God is Love, God is Great, I am God.

My divine contemplation:

My divine insight:

My divine image:

I are.

God is All, God is One, God is Love, God is Great, I am God.

My divine contemplation:

My divine insight:

My divine image:

He is Us.

God is All, God is One, God is Love, God is Great, I am God.

My divine contemplation:

My divine insight:

My divine image:

Generation One.

God is All, God is One, God is Love, God is Great, I am God.

My divine contemplation:

My divine insight:

My divine image:

God is heads, soul is tails.

God is All, God is One, God is Love, God is Great, I am God.

My divine contemplation:

My divine insight:

My divine image:

God is head and tail.

God is All, God is One, God is Love, God is Great, I am God.

My divine contemplation:

My divine insight:

My divine image:

Awareness meets God halfway.

God is All, God is One, God is Love, God is Great, I am God.

My divine contemplation:

My divine insight:

My divine image:

I am God's favorite pair of blue jeans.

God is All, God is One, God is Love, God is Great, I am God.

My divine contemplation:

My divine insight:

My divine image:

I smile, therefore, I am.

God is All, God is One, God is Love, God is Great, I am God.

My divine contemplation:

My divine insight:

My divine image:

I am Knowledge.

God is All, God is One, God is Love, God is Great, I am God.

My divine contemplation:

My divine insight:

My divine image:

I am Heart.

God is All, God is One, God is Love, God is Great, I am God.

My divine contemplation:

My divine insight:

My divine image:

I am the whole kit, cat and caboodle.

God is All, God is One, God is Love, God is Great, I am God.

My divine contemplation:

My divine insight:

My divine image:

All dreams are of me.

God is All, God is One, God is Love, God is Great, I am God.

My divine contemplation:

My divine insight:

My divine image:

God is dreaming me up.

God is All, God is One, God is Love, God is Great, I am God.

My divine contemplation:

My divine insight:

My divine image:

I am a family of one.

God is All, God is One, God is Love, God is Great, I am God.

My divine contemplation:

My divine insight:

My divine image:

Ego is the sweatshop of Love.

God is All, God is One, God is Love, God is Great, I am God.

My divine contemplation:

My divine insight:

My divine image:

God is the production line of Love.

God is All, God is One, God is Love, God is Great, I am God.

My divine contemplation:

My divine insight:

My divine image:

All stories are about me.

God is All, God is One, God is Love, God is Great, I am God.

My divine contemplation:
My divine insight:
My divine image:

God is my real name.

God is All, God is One, God is Love, God is Great, I am God.

My divine contemplation:
My divine insight:
My divine image:

Perfect 20/20 vision.

God is All, God is One, God is Love, God is Great, I am God.

My divine contemplation:

My divine insight:

My divine image:

Back to square One.

God is All, God is One, God is Love, God is Great, I am God.

My divine contemplation:

My divine insight:

My divine image:

.

Soul is divine blood cell.

God is All, God is One, God is Love, God is Great, I am God.

My divine contemplation:

My divine insight:

My divine image:

I am every word.

God is All, God is One, God is Love, God is Great, I am God.

My divine contemplation:

My divine insight:

My divine image:

The Love gene.

God is All, God is One, God is Love, God is Great, I am God.

My divine contemplation:

My divine insight:

My divine image:

I am divine DNA.

God is All, God is One, God is Love, God is Great, I am God.

My divine contemplation:

My divine insight:

My divine image:

I am a divine stem cell.

God is All, God is One, God is Love, God is Great, I am God.

My divine contemplation:

My divine insight:

My divine image:

All intelligence is artificial.

God is All, God is One, God is Love, God is Great, I am God.

My divine contemplation:

My divine insight:

My divine image:

God is seeing through my eyes.

God is All, God is One, God is Love, God is Great, I am God.

My divine contemplation:

My divine insight:

My divine image:

One head is better than two.

God is All, God is One, God is Love, God is Great, I am God.

My divine contemplation:

My divine insight:

My divine image:

I am seamless.

God is All, God is One, God is Love, God is Great, I am God.

My divine contemplation:

My divine insight:

My divine image:

All entries in the dictionary define God.

God is All, God is One, God is Love, God is Great, I am God.

My divine contemplation:

My divine insight:

My divine image:

Hallelume.

God is All, God is One, God is Love, God is Great, I am God.

My divine contemplation:

My divine insight:

My divine image:

Love is harvest.

God is All, God is One, God is Love, God is Great, I am God.

My divine contemplation:

My divine insight:

My divine image:

God even exists in forgetfulness.

God is All, God is One, God is Love, God is Great, I am God.

My divine contemplation:

My divine insight:

My divine image:

Faith is unity.

God is All, God is One, God is Love, God is Great, I am God.

My divine contemplation:

My divine insight:

My divine image:

God is meditating me.

God is All, God is One, God is Love, God is Great, I am God.

My divine contemplation:

My divine insight:

My divine image:

I am an insight gained by God contemplating Love.

God is All, God is One, God is Love, God is Great, I am God.

My divine contemplation:

My divine insight:

My divine image:

I am a temple in which God worships.

God is All, God is One, God is Love, God is Great, I am God.

My divine contemplation:

My divine insight:

My divine image:

The State of Metaphor-less-ness.

God is All, God is One, God is Love, God is Great, I am God.

My divine contemplation:
My divine insight:
My divine image:

You know the end of the movie.

God is All, God is One, God is Love, God is Great, I am God.

My divine contemplation:

My divine insight:

My divine image:

God is software and hardware.

God is All, God is One, God is Love, God is Great, I am God.

My divine contemplation:

My divine insight:

My divine image:

God is nude.

God is All, God is One, God is Love, God is Great, I am God.

My divine contemplation:

My divine insight:

My divine image:

God is recyclable (God recycles).

God is All, God is One, God is Love, God is Great, I am God.

My divine contemplation:

My divine insight:

My divine image:

Love is the only reason why.

God is All, God is One, God is Love, God is Great, I am God.

My divine contemplation:

My divine insight:

My divine image:

I give birth to myself.

God is All, God is One, God is Love, God is Great, I am God.

My divine contemplation:

My divine insight:

My divine image:

The moon is always full.

God is All, God is One, God is Love, God is Great, I am God.

My divine contemplation:

My divine insight:

My divine image:

Love is the only eternally renewable resource.

God is All, God is One, God is Love, God is Great, I am God.

My divine contemplation:
My divine insight:
My divine image:

There is no goodbye.

God is All, God is One, God is Love, God is Great, I am God.

My divine contemplation:

My divine insight:

My divine image:

Intuition is God giving Himself a hint.

God is All, God is One, God is Love, God is Great, I am God.

My divine contemplation:
My divine insight:
My divine image:

alONE

God is All, God is One, God is Love, God is Great, I am God.

My divine contemplation:
My divine insight:
My divine image:

I am a tip of the divine iceberg.

God is All, God is One, God is Love, God is Great, I am God.

My divine contemplation:

My divine insight:

My divine image:

God has no choice.

God is All, God is One, God is Love, God is Great, I am God.

My divine contemplation:

My divine insight:

My divine image:

There is here.

God is All, God is One, God is Love, God is Great, I am God.

My divine contemplation:

My divine insight:

My divine image:

I am everywhere.

God is All, God is One, God is Love, God is Great, I am God.

My divine contemplation:

My divine insight:

My divine image:

God is a paintbrush.

God is All, God is One, God is Love, God is Great, I am God.

My divine contemplation:

My divine insight:

My divine image:

All the world's a player and I am the stage.

God is All, God is One, God is Love, God is Great, I am God.

My divine contemplation:

My divine insight:

My divine image:

Only the ego can be a friend.

God is All, God is One, God is Love, God is Great, I am God.

My divine contemplation:

My divine insight:

My divine image:

God is a bachelor.

God is All, God is One, God is Love, God is Great, I am God.

My divine contemplation:

My divine insight:

My divine image:

The Truth is found at room temperature.

God is All, God is One, God is Love, God is Great, I am God.

My divine contemplation:

My divine insight:

My divine image:

I trade myself.

God is All, God is One, God is Love, God is Great, I am God.

My divine contemplation:

My divine insight:

My divine image:

The present has always been.

God is All, God is One, God is Love, God is Great, I am God.

My divine contemplation:

My divine insight:

My divine image:

I am always doing my best.

God is All, God is One, God is Love, God is Great, I am God.

My divine contemplation:

My divine insight:

My divine image:

I comprise the formula for self-realization.

God is All, God is One, God is Love, God is Great, I am God.

My divine contemplation:

My divine insight:

My divine image:

Serving others is serving myself.

God is All, God is One, God is Love, God is Great, I am God.

My divine contemplation:

My divine insight:

My divine image:

Home is where God is.

God is All, God is One, God is Love, God is Great, I am God.

My divine contemplation:

My divine insight:

My divine image:

I am always home.

God is All, God is One, God is Love, God is Great, I am God.

My divine contemplation:

My divine insight:

My divine image:

Carrying your learning forward:

I hope that contemplating and journaling the statements in The Jig Is Up, God! 108 mind-blowing, consciousness-blasting, awareness-expanding, self-realizing, ego-reducing spiritual hacks workbook has brought you joy and understanding.

Keep going. Don't stop. Continue contemplating, journaling your insights, expressing yourself through images, and documenting your experiences. Cultivate your spiritual skills by studying spiritual texts, singing the glory of God, your Self, and serving humanity by sharing the divine Love that eternally dwells in your Heart.

Remember, you are One, you are All, you are Love, you are Great and you are God!

The Jig Is Up, God! Spiritual Journal and Workbook is also available in other *original* covers, each designed by a different artist!

.